MEMORY SKILLS IN BUSINESS

by Madelyn Burley-Allen

A FIFTY-MINUTE™ SERIES BOOK

CRISP PUBLICATIONS, INC.
Menlo Park, California

MEMORY SKILLS
IN BUSINESS

by Madelyn Burley-Allen

CREDITS
Editor: **Michael G. Crisp**
Designer: **Carol Harris**
Typesetting: **Interface Studio**
Cover Design: **Carol Harris**
Artwork: **Ralph Mapson**

Copyright © 1988 by Crisp Publications, Inc.
Printed in the United States of America

http://www.crisp-pub.com

Distribution to the U.S. Trade:

National Book Network, Inc.
4720 Boston Way
Lanham, MD 20706
1-800-462-6420

Library of Congress Catalog Card Number 88-70089
Burley-Allen, Madelyn
Memory Skills in Business
ISBN 0-931961-56-4

This book is printed on recyclable paper with soy ink.

LEARNING OBJECTIVES FOR:

MEMORY SKILLS IN BUSINESS

The objectives for *Memory Skills In Business* are listed below. They have been developed to guide you, the reader, to the core issues covered in this book.

Objectives

❑ 1) To explain the capabilities of the brain.

❑ 2) To present key functions of memory systems.

❑ 3) To give practice in selecting appropriate memory systems.

Assessing Your Progress

In addition to the Learning Objectives, Crisp, Inc. has developed an **assessment** that covers the fundamental information presented in this book. A twenty-five item, multiple choice/true-false questionnaire allows the reader to evaluate his or her comprehension of the subject matter. An answer sheet with a summary matching the questions to the listed objectives is also available. To learn how to obtain a copy of this assessment please call: **1-800-442-7477** and ask to speak with a Customer Service Representative.

ABOUT THE AUTHOR

Madelyn Burley-Allen, founder of Dynamics of Human Behavior, author of three books, and author of numerous articles in various publications, holds a Master's Degree in Speech Communication at San Francisco University, in addition to Bachelor's Degrees in Developmental Psychology and Speech Communication. She is completing her doctoral program in Human Resource Development. She has received achievement awards, conducted seminars throughout the countries, and is a frequent guest speaker for state and national conferences.

ABOUT THE SERIES

With over 200 titles in print, the acclaimed Crisp 50-Minute™ series presents self-paced learning at its easiest and best. These comprehensive self-study books for business or personal use are filled with exercises, activities, assessments, and case studies that capture your interest and increase your understanding.

Other Crisp products, based on the 50-Minute books, are available in a variety of learning style formats for both individual and group study, including audio, video, CD-ROM, and computer-based training.

PREFACE

Memory systems date back to antiquity. In ancient times memory was vitally important since there was no written language. It was memory techniques and systems that enabled storytellers to remember stories, poems and songs, and orators to remember their speeches.

The importance of a memory system has not lost its importance over the centuries. Today, anyone wanting to be effective in his or her job must develop and exercise an efficient memory. Most jobs require us to store millions of pieces of information. We must have immediate mental access to company procedures, systems, products and services. We must also be aware of similar items from our competitors.

We need to remember countless names and faces and relevant facts about people with whom we meet and interact. Added to this, we are asked to accurately remember information discussed in meetings, during dozens of transactions and a variety of other details. We are, in fact, a walking computer.

Most of us use only a fraction of our memory capability. The way we improve our memory is not by improving intelligence or mental capacity, but by actively applying the fundamental principles of memory improvement and using the variety of memory techniques and systems similar to those presented in this book.

TO THE READER

How often have you wished that you were better able to remember details or experiences and then apply these memories to the task at hand? When you *are* able to recall pertinent knowledge to solve a problem, come up with a new idea or answer a complex question, you are skillfully applying your memory.

Our mind is a vast reservoir of integrated holigraphic systems composed of over 10 billion nerve cells. Scientists have scarcely tapped the surface of understanding how the human mind works. Although much has been learned, the nature of how memory functions still has many mysteries. Despite how little is really known, understanding how memory works and developing proven memory techniques will provide numerous personal and professional benefits.

Memory is a powerful mechanism hidden within you that can be tapped. Methods in this book will show you the way. Applying the techniques presented will be your key to a better memory.

No such thing as ''poor'' memory exists for most of us. The real issue is whether we have a trained memory or an untrained memory. Almost anyone who wants to improve his or her memory can use proven methods which will train the mind for better recall.

During the past fifteen years, thousands of people have improved their memories in a one-day memory improvement seminar which I conduct. Topics covered in this seminar are the basis of this book. Your memory will become increasingly trained if you repeatedly use the principles and techniques presented in this book.

Good luck,

Madelyn Burley-Allen

CONTENTS

GETTING STARTED
BACKGROUND/OVERVIEW

This book is for people who want to better remember information in a variety of situations, especially work. In every work day, we are presented with hundreds of opportunities to remember. Whether attending meetings, following directions and instructions, participating in training or other learning situations, involved in project discussions or talking one-on-one with our boss, customer or colleague, good memory skills enhance our professional image and increase productivity.

Improved memory will add to your job satisfaction. It feels good when you are able to recall the main points made at an important staff meeting. How often have you admired a person who was able to summarize what you said after you gave some complicated directions? When that person communicated back what you intended to say he probably made a positive impression and you respected his ability to remember. On the negative side, it can be frustrating when one of your colleagues forgot about a meeting you were conducting or couldn't recall your name. People who routinely forget are looked upon in disfavor. Poor memory skills can inhibit career advancement because the organization will suffer if employees do not remember well.

In this book a variety of memory strategies, mnemonics, and other techniques will be covered. Separate sections will be devoted to:

- General Principles of Memory Improvement

- Powers of Observation

- Methods to Improve Your Concentration

- Visualizing and Imaging Information to Increase Your Memory

- Keys to Association, Substitution and Linking

- Classification as a Memory Technique

- Memory Pegs for Better Recall

- A Number Recall System

BACKGROUND/OVERVIEW
(Continued)

A person with good memory skills is an asset to any work group, whereas a poor memory is usually considered a liability. Practicing what you learn in this book can help you become an asset to your organization and improve your personal productivity.

By completing the exercises in this book, you will remember names, numbers and abstract information with greater ease and assurance. Facts and data from meetings will be recalled in greater detail. Over time an improved memory will result in less misunderstanding, fewer errors, and an ability to retrieve facts which will lead to better decisions.

PART I—MEMORY DEFINED

Memory is a skill. Like any skill, it can be improved with practice. With the right attitude, you can have fun learning to improve your ability to remember. You'll be surprised how fast you will increase what you remember with practice.

Memory is nothing more than the storage and retrieval of information. In humans it is an information processing system consisting of three functions—sensory registers, short-term memory and long-term memory.

The sensory registers accept information from sensory organs (our eyes, nose, ears, etc.) and hold the information for only a few seconds. Because the sensory register time is so brief (less than five seconds normally), information has to be placed in storage for a conscious mental process to take place. Information received from the sensory register is first processed into short term memory and depending on the situation, either forgotten or sent to long-term memory. Short term memory maintains storage of information for only about 15 seconds unless something is done to capture it in long term storage.

During the course of this book, you will learn techniques which will help you maintain more information in your short-term memory. You will learn the importance of attending and focusing on what you *want* to remember and then acquire strategies such as, visualizing, associating, or substituting to recall and store greater amounts of information in short-term and long-term memory.

The final and most important objective in memory training is learning to improve your long-term memory. Experts believe that the human brain has an unlimited capacity for retaining information. However, what is remembered and how much of it can be recalled is determined by how we store and process the information. The various mnemonic (memory device) techniques you will be learning will help you increase the efficiency and effectiveness when you selectively transfer information from your sensory register, through short-term and into your long term memory.

MEMORY DEFINED
(Continued)

These three structures and functions (sensory registers, short and long term memory) are continually at work. For example, a non-technical individual will probably have difficulty registering technical information so it can be stored properly in the short-term memory. Because of limited experience with technical data, the information would be poorly transferred to the long-term memory and probably incorrectly recalled when needed.

Think about being asked to recall information the next time you attend a meeting or listen to a discussion. Normally when you hear material that is personally not interesting or downright boring, you will not remember it. If instead, you make a point to pay attention and find a reason why you should be interested in this material, you'll be surprised by how much better you remember it. You will be impressed about how much is retained and who knows, you might even learn something new!

ELEVEN PRINCIPLES FOR IMPROVED MEMORY

GENERAL PRINCIPLES FOR MEMORY IMPROVEMENT

To improve your memory there are some general principles that are required if you want to train yourself to remember more effectively. The following eleven principles will help you understand factors that are essential to memory improvement.

As this book progresses, we will expand on these individual items. For openers however, quickly review the following general principles for memory improvement.

Memory can be improved through:

1. INTEREST

It is much easier to remember things that are of interest. Interest helps you store and process information in such a way that you will remember it for a long time. This principle is extremely important. For instance, take a moment to think about something that you are genuinely interested in (i.e. sports, music, cars, gardening, another person, etc.). As you think about your interest, it will be easy to have a rush of information flooding your memory. You should be able to talk at length about your interest and remember items about it in great detail!

Now think of something that does not interest you, such as bull frogs, ditch diggers, or a speech by a long-winded politician. It is not surprising when very little information is recalled.

2. SELECTION

By choosing the most significant points about an issue, there is no need to remember everything in detail. Select what you want to remember and it will be possible to recall it a month, a year, or even five years from now. Next time you're in a situation at work where you are overwhelmed by information, pay attention to this principle of selection:
  A. Select only the information you think is most important.
  B. Take notes on this information.
  C. Ask others to review what you selected as most important and write a brief summary report from your notes.
Chances are you will remember the main point for a long time.

3. ATTENTION

Pay attention to what you want to remember. Attending to one thing at a time will help you clarify the task or event. Inattention due to lack of interest or poor concentration will impede your memory. Often people have a problem with attention because of stress or tension. Stress causes your mind to wander and not focus on what you need to remember. This is not uncommon when a student is preparing for a final exam and is overwhelmed by the task.

If you find your mind wandering because you feel stressed:
  A. Take a short break.
  B. Close your eyes and think about your favorite vacation spot for three minutes.
  C. Return to the job at hand and take things one step at a time.

GENERAL PRINCIPLES
FOR MEMORY IMPROVEMENT (Continued)

4. UNDERSTANDING

It is easier to learn and remember something when it is understood. The more new information can be associated with something you already know, the more meaning it will have. Learning something means you understand it well enough to inform others about it. Often we don't like to let on we haven't understood what is being discussed because we don't want to appear stupid. Since understanding something is critical for memory it is important to:

A. Stay prepared by reading about topics that will be discussed.
B. Keep abreast of issues by discussing them with others.
C. Ask for clarification when you don't understand.

5. INTENTION TO REMEMBER

We are more likely to recall something when we *intend* to remember it. When this happens, it increases our "original awareness." It helps when we concentrate and observe with the purpose of remembering information for a long period of time. The next time you are reading a report, read with a purpose. Note the most important point covered in each paragraph. Play a game with yourself. In each remembering situation consciously keep track of how many things you remember. By doing this over a period of time, you will develop a habit of "intending to remember."

6. CONFIDENCE: POSITIVE MENTAL SET

Without having confidence in our ability to remember, our "will" to remember becomes nothing more than a mere hope. If you use positive affirmations and visualize yourself remembering information, it will happen. Studies show that making a presentation is an activity most people fear. Many feel they can't perform very well because they might "forget." This kind of negative mental set often becomes self-fulfilling prophecy and results in poor memory.

Confidence plays a critical part in overcoming self-defeating thoughts. The next time you want to be more confident in a situation where you need to give an oral report, you should:

A. Recite your material aloud in front of a mirror. Practice it until you are comfortable with the final result.
B. Expect to remember. Believe you can deliver your speech with dynamic confidence.
C. Visualize yourself easily remembering your speech while you quickly verbalize the material.

GENERAL PRINCIPLES
FOR MEMORY IMPROVEMENT (Continued)

7. EGO INVOLVEMENT

Much of what we experience falls in one of two categories: things that please us (or we agree with) or things that displease us (or we disagree with). We seem to learn best when material reinforces our strengths, opinions or beliefs. Negative ego involvement can have serious consequences on how much is remembered. When someone discusses something that is displeasing to us, we often filter out what is displeasing and only partially hear (and remember) what was said.

This happens during meetings when emotional subjects are discussed. Think about meetings you have attended when people came away with different interpretations of what was said. The following suggestions will help you remember better, even when your ego involvement is negative.

    A. Be aware when your ego involvement is negative.
    B. Hold back your criticism.
    C. Concentrate on what the person says, not on your pre-determined biases about that person.
    D. Mentally summarize what has been said when the presentation is over.

8. ASSOCIATION

When you connect things in your mind, it is normally because they have something in common. By thinking over experiences and systematically relating and communicating them to something we already know makes it easier to remember new information. You can use mind maps to help you associate and remember information. For example, whenever you are in a meeting, or discussing a project, or talking on the phone, mind maps similar to the examples shown below can help you remember:

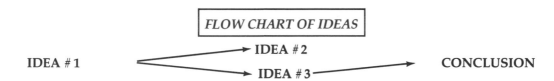

GENERAL PRINCIPLES
FOR MEMORY IMPROVEMENT (Continued)

9. BACKGROUND OF EXPERIENCE

It is important to have background experience or knowledge to help form associations. It can be difficult to understand anything that stands alone. Isolated events have limited meaning. One way to improve your memory about a subject is to learn more about the background of that subject. For example, the limited background you have received thus far from reading this book has improved your knowledge about how the memory works and your ability to form associations.

For example, list five things you've learned thus far about memory from this book:

1. _____
2. _____
3. _____
4. _____
5. _____

10. ORGANIZATION/CLASSIFICATION

There is an innate tendency of most human minds toward organization. The mind creates criteria for learning a set of related facts and makes associations between items on the basis of similarities or differences, or organizes facts into logical groups while relating these groups to each other as part of a larger grouping, etc. Classification is an important aid in remembering. When you visualize what you want to remember by classifying and organizing items, you are helping prepare the information for your long term memory. You can cluster information by using mind maps similar to those shown below:

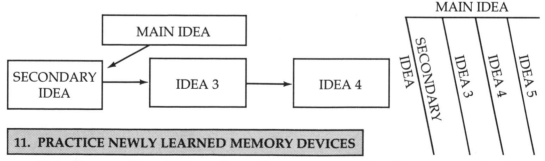

11. PRACTICE NEWLY LEARNED MEMORY DEVICES

Unless we practice techniques that we learn, our memory will stay untrained and will not improve. Memory is like any other skill (playing tennis, learning a foreign language, driving a car, etc.). The more that skill is practiced, the more improvement will occur. Take time each day to practice at least one of the memory devices you will learn in this book. To help you practice these memory devices you might want to write the eleven principles of memory just presented on 3 X 5 cards. You can then carry these with you and rehearse them when you are waiting in line, or at your leisure.

REVIEW OF ELEVEN
MEMORY IMPROVEMENT PRINCIPLES

1. **Interest**—It is much easier to remember things that interest you.

2. **Selection**—Choose significant points and concentrate on them.

3. **Attention**—Pay attention to what you want to remember.

4. **Understanding**—The better you understand new information, the easier it will be to remember it.

5. **Intention to Remember**—We can force ourselves to remember. The more we intend to remember, the easier our recall will be.

6. **Confidence: Positive Mental Set**—Visualize yourself remembering and it will happen.

7. **Ego Involvement**—Don't allow your ego to block information you may need to remember.

8. **Association**—Connect items for better memory.

9. **Background of Experience**—The more experience on a subject, the easier it is to remember new information.

10. **Organization**—Classify items into logical groupings.

11. **Practice Newly Learned Memory Devices**—The more you practice memory techniques, the better your memory will become.

THE BRAIN HAS AN UNLIMITED CAPACITY
TO REMEMBER FACTS AND FIGURES

THE BRAIN AND ITS POTENTIAL

In relation to memory, it is important to understand the potential of a human brain. A negative view of our ability to remember will interfere with our memory potential. Learning just how incredible our brain is will help you view the potential you have to remember more positively.

Brains are often compared to computers. Brains however are much more impressive! What computer could appreciate Mozart, discover abstract principles, or feel happy, angry or bored? Especially a computer the size of a cantaloup?

Human memory is organized not just alphabetically, numerically and topically but in innumerable other ways. Items are arranged in millions of interlacing networks. The result is that practically any word, image or previous event can be reached from any starting point by a vast number of routes. Knowledge in the memory network is packaged in stereotypical routines of clusters of well known cause-in-effect relationships.

William James said many years ago, and most scientists today still agree that we use less than 10% of our brain power! Think what your life would be like if you used just 20% of your brain's potential!

A human brain has over 100 *billion* working parts. Most brains weigh just over 3 pounds and contain between 10 and 14 billion neuron cells. To visualize how tiny these cells are, 250,000 of them will fit on a penny. Yet, each of those tiny cells is capable of storing between one and two million bits of information. The storage capacity of a brain equals ten new items every second, for a lifetime. That means a potential for 600 new items per minute or 36,000 bits of information in an hour. For a normal lifetime, a human brain has the capacity to store more than 100 trillion bits of information.

Another example is that an average adult's memory has the potential to hold at least 500 times as much information as is in an entire set of the *Encyclopedia Britannica*. Even at a young age memory is impressive. By the age of three, a human mind can connect events long before they can be dealt with verbally. For instance, you couldn't fit into the most sophisticated computer all of what a four year old knows about his or her mother's kitchen. The brain is truly a small universe unto itself.

THE BRAIN AND ITS POTENTIAL
(Continued)

Our minds come equipped with highly efficient neural arrangements that have been built through evolution. These predispose us to make sense out of our experiences and use them in that distinctly human activity we call thinking.

Each brain has over ten billion nerve fibers which give out electrical impulses. Each nerve cell has thousands of inputs and outputs to other cells throughout the entire body. In biological terms, the "single switch" is a synapse. This is a junction where a nerve cell can transmit its message to a second nerve cell or a muscle. The marvel of the synapse is its ability to translate electrical energy into chemical energy and back again. When an electrical impulse is sent down a nerve fiber, chemicals called neurotransmitters are released. If these neurotransmitters reach a second neuron that has the right receptors on its surface, they cause a reaction that carries on the electrical nerve impulse in the second neuron. If released onto a muscle, this impulse will cause it to contract. This whole process of transmitter release takes less than one thousandth of a second. It is theorized that the synapse becomes stronger when it is used more often and weaker when it is used less, thus "exercising the brain" is not just an idle phrase.

Your brain allows choice based on experience and expectation. This means that the more you experience things, the more you acquire knowledge, the greater probability you will increase the potential use of your brain. Your expectations strongly influence how you utilize your brain. If you expect little to be achieved, that's what you are going to get.

Your brain is a biological, electrical switchboard that is a link between the inner being and the lifeform it is occupying. Mere consciousness is not awareness. Consciousness is of the physical brain, while awareness is of the mind. Consciousness combined with a higher awareness tells each human being, "I am a living, thinking and unique individual."

THE HISTORY OF MEMORY SYSTEMS

Memory systems have been around for all of recorded history. Greek and Roman orators delivered lengthy speeches with unfailing accuracy. They learned these speeches, thought by thought, by applying a memory system technique of association and imagery.

Simonides (500 B.C.) is regarded as "father" of the art of trained memory. He saw memory training as an essential part of an orator's equipment. Scraps of parchment dating back a thousand years before Simonides make mention of the importance of a trained memory, so memory training has been around a long time.

Ancients knew that memory training helped the thinking process. From a document dated 400 B.C. we learn that "A great and beautiful invention is memory, always useful both for learning and for life." Aristotle, after praising memory systems said that "These habits too will make a man readier in reasoning."

St. Thomas Acquinas, a patron saint, was instrumental in making the art of trained memory a devotional and ethical art. During the Middle Ages, monks and philosophers were virtually the only people who applied trained memory techniques.

In 1491, Peter of Ravenna wrote "The Phoenix" which is the best known of all early memory books and brought trained memory into the lay world. King Francis I of France used memory systems. Henry III of England also did. Shakespeare used trained memory systems in his Globe Theater called "memory theatre."

Philosophers in the 17th Century taught memory systems. Francis Bacon has one in his book, "The Advancement of Learning." Some scholars insist that Leibniz invented calculus while searching for a memory system that would aid in memorizing numbers.

All of the systems used by these famous people were based on observation, association and visualization. They understood that individuals must observe and visualize before they can recall what is to be remembered. The first **Key Function of Memory** is knowing how to observe which you will learn more about by turning this page.

ONE KEY TO A BETTER MEMORY
IS LEARNING HOW TO CONCENTRATE

PART II—MEMORY SYSTEMS

This section of MEMORY SKILLS IN BUSINESS will cover the major memory systems and/or techniques as well as items contributing to memory. Following is a list of items covered in Part II:

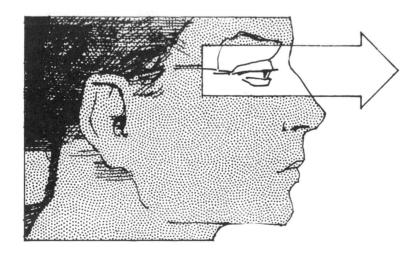

KEY FUNCTION #1
OBSERVATION

HOW GOOD ARE YOUR POWERS OF OBSERVATION?

There are three items shown on the facing page. Study each briefly and then, based on your observation, write what you noticed about each item in the space provided:

ITEM 1 _____

_____

_____

ITEM 2 _____

_____

_____

ITEM 3 _____

_____

_____

Look more closely at page 17. Did you observe that each item represented or contained a word? Item #1 was easy. Most of you probably recognized the word triangular. What about item #2? Did you observe the word squares? Or, most difficult of all, find the word *hidden* in the midst of the letters in item #3?

To improve your memory, it is critical that you develop your ability to observe. Most often we neglect to practice the habit of careful observation. When we don't keenly observe an event, our memory won't register it in such a way we can recall it later. If we are not in the habit of paying attention to detail much will escape us.

Don't feel discouraged if you didn't do as well as you thought you might. Your powers of observation can be increased by putting into practice the principles and techniques in this book.

The more you observe by being aware, the more you will remember. Just seeing is not enough. It is necessary to concentrate on what you are observing and fix your attention on the matter at hand.

THREE ITEMS *

1.

```
        T
      R I
    A N G
  U L A R
```

2.

3.

C S K Y V E N U Q M

V M N F O L T E I P

A J H I D D E N G R

P Q S U O T W X B K

N F L Z R G M J O H

* Adapted from *WORDS*, William Kaufmann, Inc., Menlo Park, California 1980.

IMPROVED CONCENTRATION EQUALS IMPROVED MEMORY

Learning concentration techniques, practicing them and training them to become habits will help you observe things more clearly, which will improve memory. Although attention spans vary from person to person—it is possible to improve concentration through mental visual exercises similar to the one below. Exercises such as these will help you improve your ability to concentrate. Following is one such exercise.

CONCENTRATION EXERCISE

Find a comfortable position. Close your eyes and become aware of your body . . . Turn your attention away from outside events and notice what is going on inside you . . . Notice any discomfort, what parts of your body seem vague and indistinct . . . If you become aware of a tense area of your body, see if you can let go of the tension . . . If not, try deliberately tensing the part, to see what muscles you are tensing . . . and then let go again . . . Focus attention on your breathing . . . Become aware of the details of your breathing . . . Feel the air move in through your nose or mouth . . . into your chest and belly following the movement as you breathe . . . Imagine your breathing is like gentle waves on the shore, and that each wave slowly washes some tension out of your body.

Next, become aware of thoughts or images that come into your mind . . . Just notice them. What are they about, and what are they like? . . . Now imagine that you put your thoughts and images into a glass jar and watch them . . . Examine them . . . What are your thoughts and images like? What do they do as you watch them? . . . As most thoughts or images come into your mind, put them into the jar too, and see what you can learn about them . . . Now take your mental jar and pour out the thoughts and images. Watch as they disappear and the jar once again is empty. . . .

Concentrate on the empty jar . . . Continue doing this for as long as you can.

When it feels right, slowly open your eyes and notice the objects around you. Take a few minutes before you begin any activity.

It is important to do this exercise at least once each day at a convenient time for you. Many people do it first thing in the morning. Most people find that this relaxation exercise helps them concentrate better throughout the day. It can be repeated prior to any situation where concentration is important.

OBSERVATION EXERCISE

A picture is shown on the next page. You will be asked to observe it for three minutes and then recall as many items as you can. There are more than thirty items shown in the picture. Take a visual picture and write down as many items as possible in the space provided

1. _____   16. _____

2. _____   17. _____

3. _____   18. _____

4. _____   19. _____

5. _____   20. _____

6. _____   21. _____

7. _____   22. _____

8. _____   23. _____

9. _____   24. _____

10. _____   25. _____

11. _____   26. _____

12. _____   27. _____

13. _____   28. _____

14. _____   29. _____

15. _____   30. _____

If you could recall 22 items, your memory is superior. If you wrote down 15 to 22, your memory is above average. From 10 to 15 items is average. Less than that number indicates you need work on learning to observe, visualize and recall. With practice you can improve. Check your list with the items on page 62. If you had items not on the list, but in the picture, good for you! Score one point for each item.

KEY FUNCTION #2
VISUALIZING/IMAGING

The second key function is the phenomenon of visualizing. It is the ability for your mind to picture an event or item. We visualize on an almost continual basis. Some of us do it more consciously than others, but we all do it. For example, try to form a mental picture of an elephant sitting on top of your house. You probably were able to do this even though the image was ridiculous and out of the realm of actual experience.

You can visualize any event so long as the scene consists of concrete, imagable objects. It is possible to imagine all sorts of scenes, even moving ones, by just thinking about it. Have you ever imagined objects when you smell an odor such as popcorn being popped or barbecue on the grill? Will the sound of a distant train whistle conjure a vision of a train speeding down the track for you? Does listening to music bring back visual memories that are associated with other experiences you may have had when that music was played? We constantly remember facts, events and experiences that we picture in our minds eye. Because we can imagine objects in a scene, we can also imagine objects interacting. It is easy to imagine a person is pushing a cart down a hall, a man running to catch a bus or a woman walking to the parking lot and getting in her car.

What is much more difficult for us to imagine is abstract information. For instance can you form an image of a loyal manager or an employee defending his or her honor?

It is fairly easy to imagine the manager and employee doing something. It is much more difficult to imagine loyalty or honor because they are abstract items. Thus, visualizing works best for concrete objects and scenes. For instance, read the following scenes and notice which you can easily picture. Put a check by the ones that are difficult to visualize.

1. ☐ A teller in a bank counting out money to a man

2. ☐ A woman admired for her creativity

3. ☐ Three people dancing on a table

4. ☐ A crowd caught up in guilt

5. ☐ Two individuals carrying a statue ten feet tall

VISUALIZING/IMAGING (Continued)

You probably discovered that items 1, 3 and 5 from the previous page were the easy items to visualize because they contained concrete descriptions. The more difficult ones (items 2 and 4) included abstract concepts. It's important to realize that concrete images form sharper pictures and are easier to remember. Thus, an important key to using visualization to assist your memory is that the more concrete your images are, the more likely you will be able to remember an item or event.

For example, consider what would happen if you were called on to remember an accident you witnessed. You would probably be able to see the accident in your mind's eye. If there was a second witness, he or she would probably see pretty much the same basic mental picture. In other words, visualization would assist each of you to remember the scene. Could either of you remember the event without creating a mental picture of it? Most likely not.

If both of you however, were asked to give details of the accident, it would be rare if you gave exactly the same description. This is because we have a tendency to interpret events based on our emotional state at the time of the event, our beliefs and our previous experiences or references. We fill in gaps where the mind is unclear or uncertain about what took place. This is something every good trial lawyer soon learns.

Many disagreements on the job (and in life) are the result of phenomenon. How often do co-workers remember things that were discussed in meetings differently than you? Meetings are often made up of abstract material, so it is more likely things can have a wider range of interpretation. In such situations, those with a reputation for having a good memory are usually consulted to establish what actually occurred.

IS YOUR MEMORY MORE VISUAL OR AUDITORY?

The ability to visualize with near 100% accuracy is called eidetic memory. The popular term for this is "photographic memory." Very few individuals are blessed with this unique talent. A noted mathematician, John Von Neumann, was such a person. According to a reporter writing in Life Magazine, Von Neumann, when eight years old, could memorize the names, addresses *and* phone numbers of an entire page in a phone directory "on sight." He retained this ability all his life and was able to carry out complex mathematical calculations in his mind. Chances are you are not an eidetic. If you are, this book can't do much for you. It was written for the other 99.99% of the world.

Some people seem to remember what they see. Others do a better job with what they hear. Regardless of which best describes you, our senses reinforce each other. Thus it is best to use both sensory modes to improve your memory. Psychologists agree that most individuals are either better at visual or auditory memorization. One psychologist, F.C. Bartlett after painstaking research of visual and auditory memorizers, characterized each as follows:

> *Visual memorizers* tend to learn rapidly and confidently. They also are confident in reproducing what they have learned. They tend to deal directly with the subject matter by visualizing it as it is presented. They depend less on grouping, comparing, or making secondary associations. Bartlett also found that "visualizers" change their material more when recalling it. They sometimes get the order of things mixed up and often introduce extraneous material. Their attitude generally is one of confidence, irrespective of objective accuracy.

> *Auditory memorizers* on the other hand tend to grasp signs or cues and then attach them with descriptions. They use classifications, associations, and comparisons to remember. In recalling an event, they tend to respond with some uncertainty, even when their memory is accurate.

Which type are you? Complete the exercise on page 25, then turn to page 63 to find out which skill is more developed. Add up your scores and see if you tend to be an audio memorizer or a visual memorizer. Regardless of whether you are more strongly visual or auditory, you should understand each type and to try to strengthen the other learning ability (visual or auditory) whichever is weaker.

HOW WELL CAN YOU CREATE MENTAL IMAGES?

Studies have shown that utilizing both senses is advantageous. Names, technical terms, and foreign language words can be learned best when you both see *and* hear them. If you only see *or* hear them, you lose the value of double learning. If you only hear them, you may have trouble with spelling. If you only see them, it may be difficult to pronounce them properly or recognize the words when others use them while speaking.

When it comes to facts and ideas, it really does not matter whether you place them in your memory through sight or hearing, (though using both is desirable). An auditory learner should spend more time reciting orally what is being read. Though oral reading is slow, an auditory learner should read aloud any difficult passages. A visualizer probably needs to take more complete notes than an auditory learner.

Now that you know how important it is to use visualization to increase what you remember, the exercise on the facing page will help determine what kind of memorizer you are.

The ability to create clear, vivid mental images varies among individuals. There is even a small percentage of the population who swear they never generate mental images. The following exercise was adapted from one created by psychologist Arnold Lazarus. It will help you measure how vivid your images really are. You need to create clear images if you plan to make imagery techniques a useful tool for improving your memory.

You can complete the exercise on the facing page in two ways. You can either have a person read the following list to you, or you can read it yourself while forming each item mentally in your mind's eye. You may keep your eyes closed or open, whichever helps you picture the item most clearly.

EXERCISE AHEAD

MENTAL IMAGE EXERCISE

Record the clarity of each item using one of the following categories:

If your image is "Extremely Clear" rate it	4
If your image is "Clear" rate it	3
If your image is "Fairly Clear" rate it	2
If your image is "Unclear" rate it	1
If your image is "Very Unclear" rate it	0

If you choose to read the list yourself, after you read the item, either look away or close your eyes to picture it in your mind. Give yourself about 30 seconds per item, then rate how clearly you were able to image the item. Complete all items.

1. Think about a close relative or friend
   a. See him/her standing in front of you _____
   b. Imagine him/her laughing _____
2. Picture a bowl of fruit _____
3. Imagine the sound of a car door slamming _____
4. Picture your childhood home _____
5. Imagine the sound of a car starting up _____
6. See a white, sandy beach _____
7. Imagine the sound of your favorite friends' voice _____
8. Imagine looking into a shop window _____
9. Hear your favorite song _____
10. See a blank television screen _____
11. Imagine the sound of a barking dog _____
12. Picture yourself sitting at your desk _____
13. Imagine the sound of an airplane _____
14. See yourself at your favorite restaurant _____
15. Imagine the sound of a fork hitting a plate _____
16. See a beautiful flower garden _____
17. Imagine a gun being fired _____

TOTAL YOUR RATINGS _____

RATING SCALE:

60 or more	You have a very well-developed power of imagery
31 to 59	Imagery techniques will be useful to you
30 or less	Imagery technique won't be highly useful without special imagery training

Now turn to page 63 to determine if you are more visual or auditory in your approach to learning.

RIGHT/LEFT HEMISPHERES OF YOUR BRAIN

To better understand how your brain works, it is critical to realize that it is composed of a left and right hemisphere. Each side is called a cerebral hemisphere and each hemisphere is specialized for different cognitive functions.

If the two hemispheres are surgically disconnected, they will continue to function as separate conscious minds in the same head. These dual aspects of our consciousness have been known for centuries.

They are like two separate minds. Because each is specialized they are different, not duplicate minds.

Two Modes of Knowing:

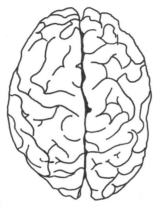

Logic	Intuition
Sequentional	Relationships
Verbal	Visual
Linear	Spacial
Analytical	Creative

Left Hemisphere

Right Hemisphere

THE RIGHT HEMISPHERE

The right hemisphere is a holistic, "gestalt" mode and handles spatial relations. The right hemisphere is intuitive and deals in thinking: It grasps the relations between the parts directly rather than by a sequence of deductions. It is primarily concerned with our simultaneous comprehension.

The right side of our brain is very good at perceiving and expressing novel complex visual, spatial and musical patterns. It is able to synthesize all this information into an understandable whole.

A person with a major right hemisphere injury would probably have trouble copying geometric figures, matching a design with wood blocks, recognizing faces or melodies. This is because these tasks require a person to keep in mind an overall pattern of relationships, not simply individual parts.

LEFT HEMISPHERES OF YOUR BRAIN
ed)

the right side of the brain likes space, observes non-verbal
ication, processes color and design, remembers faces and impressions,
music, and has artistic talents. Music is analyzed in the auditory region of
th. hemisphere.

This holistic method of information processing is very good for bridging gaps. A
"right brain" person can perceive a pattern even when some of the pieces are
missing. In this imperfect world, we are often operating with incomplete
information. It is important for us to have the capacity to perceive general patterns
and jump across gaps.

THE LEFT HEMISPHERE

The left hemisphere is the logical mode. It controls analytic thought and verbal
responses.

The left side of the brain deals with information in a linear, logical way which
operates in a piecemeal, step-by-step process. It is specialized for spoken
language, reading and writing. This verbal-analytic style is extremely efficient for
dealing with the object world. Because the left hemisphere proceeds in a logical,
sequential mode, it cannot skip over gaps. Spoken words are individually
analyzed in the auditory region of this hemisphere.

Therefore, a "left brain" person likes words, information and numbers, that
move in a linear, logical order.

Our modern technology, standard of living and scientific achievement depend
heavily on highly developed linear, analytic methods.

THE TWO HEMISPHERES TOGETHER

The two hemispheres can operate in a complementary or conflicting manner.
Analytic and holistic modes are complimentary when each provides a dimension
that the other lacks. The two modes can be in conflict when there is some mutual
antagonism between them, such as the tendency of the left hemisphere to note
details in a form suitable for expression.

Creativity occurs when there is a smooth integration between both hemispheres
of the brain. It is important to help the development of both modes so you can
use them more effectively. By practicing and applying the powers of observation,
concentration, classification and memory pegs you can strengthen and develop
your left hemisphere function.

Memory devices such as visualizing, association, linking and substitution will
help increase your ability to use your right hemisphere.

Putting both forms of memory devices into practice in your daily life will help you
gradually increase your creative abilities.

KEY FUNCTION #3
MEMORY ASSOCIATION

The next key function of memory training (that uses visualization) is the process of association. Association and imaging interact continuously. This occurs because whatever appears in the mind must be introduced, and associated with something already there. Your memory depends on an organized system of association.

All memory (trained or untrained) is based on association. Perhaps the single most important way to remember information is to associate it with something you already know. This process helps keep you aware of the information you want to remember. It increases and improves your awareness and observation of what you want to remember. Thus, your original awareness is initiated. Anything of which you are originally aware is more difficult to forget. When you apply a system of association it forces original awareness. Observation is essential to original awareness. Anything you wish to remember must be first observed using association to assist you.

If you take a new piece of information and associate it with something you already know, it is easier to remember the new information. Thus, of two people with same experience and education, the one who thinks about his or her experiences and weaves them into a systematic relationship with each other, will have the better memory.

One method that can help train you to associate items is by asking the questons why, when, how, where, who. When a new item you wish to remember is brought up ask these key questions.

- **WHY** is this so?
- **WHEN** would it be so?
- **HOW** is it so?
- **WHERE** is this so?
- **WHO** said it is so?

Answering these questions will help you form a complete picture of the item and help you remember it. You will learn what there is to know about the situation, and then may accept or reject it. You'll find that when issues are supported by answers to these key questions, they will stay in your memory.

Rudyard Kipling, in *The Elephant's Child*, said:

"I keep six honest serving men

(They taught me all I knew);

Their names are What and Why and When

And How and Where and Who"

Everyone uses association. The problem is that often it is done subconsciously without recognizing that it is a memory enhancing process.

A BASIC MEMORY RULE

You can remember any new piece of information more easily if you can associate it with something you already know. For example:

- To remember the notes in the treble clef of a musical staff—learn the sentence, **E**very **G**ood **B**oy **D**oes **F**ine (E. G, B. D, F).

- To spell the word piece—think of the phrase, ''a *piece* of *pie*.''

- To recall the shape of Italy — think of a boot.

Memory aides (often called mnemonics) such as the above examples can help you remember items, even if they involve unfamiliar or abstract concepts or names.

Tips to keep in mind to use Association effectively for greater memory:

- Associate new information to something you already know

- Keep your powers of observation working at all time to be originally aware

- Ask why, when, how, where and who

- Visualize what you want to remember

- Apply memory aides—Mnemonics

KEY FUNCTION #4
SUBSTITUTION

Almost every day at your job there is a need to remember abstract material. This can be information discussed in meetings, concepts covered in training situations or new technical information that you read. As previously mentioned, abstract information is more difficult to remember because it is not easy to readily imagine a picture of what is being learned. One way to overcome this is to use a "substitute word." The substitute word concept can be applied to almost any abstract material.

When you hear or see a word that seems abstract or intangible, think of anything that *sounds* like or *reminds* you of the abstraction you want to remember. Anything that can be *pictured* in your mind will do. Often, the name of a person, thing or place cannot be pictured in your mind. Most names are intangible, which is one reason they are so difficult to remember. For instance, if you want to remember Minnesota or Leslie you could do this:

Minnesota—mini soda, a small bottle of soda

Leslie—the salt company

You have to use your *imagination.* The more you form conscious associations the easier it will become. You will be improving your imagination as you improve your memory.

EXAMPLE: How could you remember the three memory functions, **Recognition**, **Reconstruction** and **Recall**? Perhaps by using a substitution memory device similar to this.

— First you might notice they all begin with the letter "R."
— Then for **Recognition** you might visualize yourself meeting someone named **Robert** whom you **Recognize**.
— For **Reconstruction** you might see **Robert's** home being **Re**-roofed as part of its **Reconstruction**.
— For **Recall** you might have imagined **Robert Returning** your *call*.

SUBSTITUTION (Continued)

It is the image making part of the mind that helps you remember things and events. The mind never thinks without forming mental pictures. No one could learn or understand anything without the faculty of forming mental images.

The key to better memory is to learn how to associate images with intangibles. Pictures, substitute words, thoughts or phrases can be used to remind you of intangible material. Trying to find a substitute word for anything forces you to think about it. It helps you concentrate on what you want to remember.

To remember the sequence of colors in the rainbow — memorize the sentence **R**ead **O**ver **Y**our **G**reek **B**ook **I**n **V**acation, (Red, Orange, Yellow, Green, Blue, Indigo, Violet).

Or another example of substitution is using the word HOMES to remember the five Great Lakes (Huron, Ontario, Michigan, Erie, Superior).

SUBSTITUTION EXERCISE

To develop substitution as a memory skill see if you can use it to remember the general principles for Memory Improvement mentioned earlier in this book (interest, selection, attention, understanding, intuition, confidence, ego, association, background, organization and practice.) Each principle is an abstract word and/or concept. Unless you developed a substitution mnemonic device you would probably try to remember these principles using a rote memory system. Rote systems are probably those you used throughout your early education since it is popular in most school systems.

By applying rote memory techniques, it would take most people fifteen to thirty minutes to remember the names of the eleven principles. However, by using a substitution mnemonic device, this time can be cut in half. Each general principle is listed below with space next to it for you to either draw a picture of an object (or person), or write the word of the object. The first principal has been completed for you to better demonstrate how substitution works.

1. **INTEREST** _____ % percentage symbol (i.e. ''I was charged 10% interest _____ on my loan.'')

2. **SELECTION** _____

3. **ATTENTION** _____

4. **UNDERSTANDING** _____

5. **INTENTION TO REMEMBER** _____

6. **CONFIDENCE: POSITIVE MENTAL SET** _____

7. **EGO** _____

8. **ASSOCIATION** _____

9. **BACKGROUND** _____

10. **ORGANIZATION** _____

11. **PRACTICE** _____

Compare what you have written with the author's response on the facing page.

AUTHOR'S RESPONSE— SUBSTITUTION EXERCISE

Following are some examples of substitution mnemonics. It doesn't matter if yours were different so long as they allowed you to visualize a substitution example which helped you remember the key word.

1. Interest — *% percentage symbol*

2. Selection — *Imagine yourself selecting an object you like such as a piece of candy from an assorted box of chocolates.*

3. Attention — *Think of a soldier standing at attention.*

4. Understanding —*Picture a person under a stand.*

5. Intention to Remember —*Imagine a person in a tent with a light bulb over his or her head.)*

6. Confidence —*Picture a person with their chest out.*

7. Ego —*See an ''E'' on top of a Go sign.*

8. Association —*Imagine an association you belong to.*

9. Background —*Think about someone lying on their back on the ground.*

10. Organization —*Picture an organization chart, or an open file drawer that is organized.*

11. Practice —*Imagine someone practicing on a musical instrument or practicing a sport.*

More than likely you found this exercise took effort. Some of you may find it difficult. This is because you are not accustomed to using the memory aide of substitution mnemonics. Like any skill you will discover that the more you use this technique the more you will be comfortable using it. One way to practice it is to draw pictures or symbols of key ideas as you listen in meetings. By practice, you'll be amazed how much easier it will be.

KEY FUNCTION #5 CLASSIFICATION

When cave people first began using words to communicate with each other, their need for language was met by sounds that stood for the places and objects of daily life. They agreed, for example, to use combinations of grunts, whistles, and clucks for CAVE, FIRE, GROUND, TREE, BROOK, LAKE and RAIN.

Over time there probably came along a cave man (or cave woman) with a scientific mind. This person discovered that BROOK, LAKE and RAIN were all alike in some ways, they were ALL GOOD TO DRINK, and ALL WOULD WET THE HAIR AND SKIN. This cave person may have invented a new combination of sounds to stand for the common properties of BROOK, LAKE and RAIN; simply known from that day forward as WATER.

This hypothetical discovery was the start of classification (or the grouping of objects which are alike.) RAIN, BROOK and LAKE all contain the common element of water.

Our primitive scientist was probably pleased to discover this concept helped make life more orderly. We can imagine that this person was also gratified to find CLASSIFICATION helped him or her to remember the names of objects that were alike. We can be sure that the method of classification (regardless of who discovered it) has helped advance civilization.

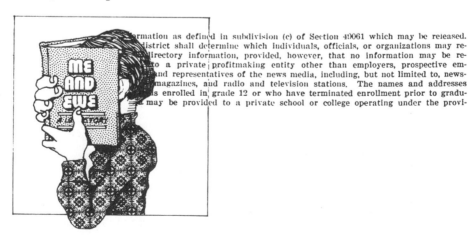

CLASSIFICATION MAKES READING EASIER TO REMEMBER

CLASSIFICATION EXERCISE

YOU also can use classification to improve YOUR memory. You can demonstrate how classification helps you to remember with a simple experiment. Look at the drawing on the next page for exactly one minute. Then try to list below all the objects shown below.

1. _____

2. _____

3. _____

4. _____

5. _____

6. _____

7. _____

8. _____

9. _____

10. _____

11. _____

12. _____

13. _____

14. _____

15. _____

16. _____

CLASSIFICATION EXERCISE (Continued)

Study this drawing for exactly one minute. Then return to page 35 to write down as many of the objects as you can remember.

CLASSIFICATION EXERCISE (Continued)

It is certainly not easy to recall all the objects in the haphazard grouping shown on the facing page. If, however, you classified the objects (as shown in the drawing below) you will probably realize there is a logical, scientific way to remember them. You see the same sixteen objects, but classification helps you remember them better.

SPORTS EQUIPMENT	OFFICE ITEMS
tennis racket	calendar
golf clubs	file cabinet
bat	calculator
football	desk

FURNITURE	MUSICAL INSTRUMENTS
couch	clarinet
armchair	guitar
table	piano
chair	violin

Whenever you deal with several items, you can make it easier by dividing them into groups. Such a division should not be done randomly. You need to insure that items in each group compliment each other and are different from items in the other groups. Since things relate to each other in different ways, it is possible to classify them in many categories. If you think for instance, of the population of a nation, it can be classified in all the following ways:

according to states, provinces, counties or territories

according to age

according to sex

according to profession or occupation

according to income

according to education

Add your own: _____

_____

_____

KEY FUNCTION #6 LINKING

Associating one thought to another is the basis of the *Link System.* A basic rule in remembering a new piece of information is that it must be associated to something you already know, or to remember it in some ridiculous way. Doing it forces an original awareness that is necessary to remember anything. Whenever you concentrate, or use *imagination,* you will be forced to consciously form associations which will aid your memory.

Assume you want to memorize the following ten items in sequence: airplane, tree, envelope, earring, bucket, sing, basketball, salami, star, nose. First you need to picture an airplane in your mind. Next, link the tree and airplane together in a ridiculous way such as an airplane growing on a tree. What you've just done is associate two things in a ridiculous way.

Two steps were involved:

First you need a ridiculous, absurd picture to associate the two items. What you don't want is a picture that is too logical or sensible.

Examples: *Ridiculous*—a tree with wings that is flying or airplanes growing on a tree.

Logical—an airplane parked near a tree.

Select one of these pictures and see it in your mind's eye. Don't simply see the airplane and tree; see them doing something together. This memory device is called the *Link System* because what you are doing is linking one item to another. In forming links of a memory chain, one item must lead you to the next, if associating correctly.

LINKING (Continued)

One problem you may have in Linking is to make your mental picture ridiculous enough. Five simple rules will help you:

1. **SUBSTITUTION**: Picture one item doing what the other does (i.e. the tree flying instead of the plane.)

2. **IMAGINE THINGS OUT OF PROPORTION**: See items larger than life, gigantic, tremendous.

3. **EXAGGERATE NUMBERS**. Instead of seeing one tree flying, think of an entire forest airborne.

4. **GET ACTION INTO YOUR PICTURES**. Use imagination like you did as a child. Children don't have trouble picturing ridiculous, silly images.

5. **MAKE UNUSUAL COMBINATIONS** such as a birch bark airplane.

Making pictures ridiculous is what enables you to remember them. Logical pictures are too vague. Once you envision a ridiculous picture, it is easier to remember.

Research conducted at the Southern California College of Optometry has shown when you actually see something, an electrical impulse travels between the vision and the brain. A similar reaction occurs when you imagine something. Surprisingly, there is not much physiological difference between electrical signals that are activated through imagination and ones that are activated by the eye itself.

You will probably have to practice to come up with ridiculous pictures but by using extra effort you can train yourself to be original and will remember things more readily.

KEY FUNCTION #7
MEMORY PEGS

One of the most effective methods for using the process of association in a systematic way is the mnemonic (nee-mon-ik) device (often called memory pegs.) This technique is important as most people haven't trained their minds to use association effectively. How many times have you heard someone say—''That reminds me . . .'' This is an example of non-controlled association.

Memory pegs will provide you with a system that can be used in a wide variety of situations. Instead of being stuck with a non-controlled association process. You can adapt the system you build. A memory peg system makes it possible for you to have an systematic arrangement of storage places in your mind in which permanent items are engraved. New thoughts, ideas or objects can then be associated to these permanent items to help you remember the new information. When you do this you simply peer into your memory bank and retrieve the information you want to remember.

How To Develop Memory Pegs

There are various ''lists'' you can develop to use as your memory pegs. People often use objects found in their homes. Memory pegs work best when they are specific objects. To qualify, an object should not be used more than once and be something you are familiar with. They also should be arranged in a logical sequence.

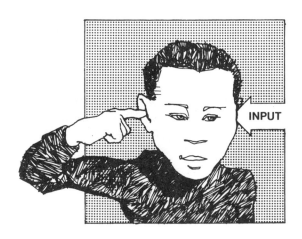

MEMORY PEGS—AN EXERCISE

In the following example and exercise you will be asked to develop 20 pegs. The reason for 20 pegs is because 10 won't stretch your ability and more than 20 is more than you probably will need.

For illustration, let's assume you select 20 household objects found in your living area. First you should draw a floor plan of your house or apartment. Next you should decide what would be the most logical sequence walk through this area. For example, it might be logical for you to start in your kitchen, then go to the dining room, living room, hall, bathroom, family room and bedroom, in that sequence. You should select objects in each room that are easiest for you to remember. For example:

In the Kitchen
    1. Refrigerator
    2. Sink

Dining Room
    3. Large buffet
    4. Chandelier

Living Room
    5. Tall lamp on end table
    6. Stereo
    7. Fireplace
    8. T.V.

Hall
    9. Front door
   10. Hall closet
   11. Large picture at the end of the hall

Bathroom
   12. Toilet
   13. Bathtub
   14. Medicine cabinet

Family Room
   15. Bay window
   16. Piano

Bedroom
   17. Jewelry box
   18. Window & oak tree
   19. Bed
   20. Dresser

MEMORY PEGS—DEVELOPING YOUR SYSTEM

In the space provided, develop 20 pegs of your own. Use any logical system as described on page 40. Remember, these will become your permanent memory pegs so you should be thoughtful about what you select.

1. _____

2. _____

3. _____   Location: _____

4. _____

5. _____

6. _____   Location: _____

7. _____

8. _____

9. _____

10. _____   Location: _____

11. _____

12. _____

13. _____

14. _____   Location: _____

15. _____

16. _____   Location: _____

17. _____

18. _____

19. _____   Location: _____

20. _____

After you have developed your list of memory peg objects, take an imaginery trip through the locations in sequence. Mentally, visualize each object as you travel through. When taking your ''walk'' see the objects in the sequence you wrote them down. If an object doesn't seem to be in the proper sequence, rearrange it until it feels right to you. Mentally review your 20 objects several times.

YOUR MEMORY PEGS

It should not take long to remember your objects in the sequence you developed them. Most people after taking the imaginary walk three to five times, find they can remember their objects in sequence.

Once you have committed your 20 objects to memory reinforce them until they are etched in your long term memory bank. Once this has been done you can use them whenever you like. This memorization should be similar to other mental frameworks you have developed such as, the multiplication table or the alphabet. Whenever you want to use your personal ''memory peg,'' just look into your long term memory and collect the information you need.

Now it's time to learn how to use your imagination to associate other items with your memory peg objects. You'll be amazed how much fun it is to remember 20 new items in the order they are listed.

A sample list is provided on the next page. By associating each item to your memory peg object, you should learn how to remember all items on the list. Once you see how it's done using the list provided, you'll be able to associate any similar list to your personal memory pegs.

EXERCISE AHEAD

MEMORY PEGS EXERCISE

Following is your sample list:

1. Blue Suit

2. Briefcase

3. Calling Cards

4. Manilla Envelope

5. Stamps

6. Expense Account Form

7. Airline Tickets

8. Joan Thompson

9. Bill Barnes

10. Acme Manufacturing Company

11. Hilton Hotel

12. Suite 100

13. 2:00 P.M. Meeting

14. 4:00 P.M. Limo

15. International Airport

16. Flight 123

17. Air Canada

18. Rental Car

19. Kon-Tiki Restaurant

20. Call Home

MEMORY PEGS EXERCISE (Continued)

Study page 44, cover it with a piece of paper, and then complete the following exercise.

Associate and imagine the first five items. Once you have associated them in order write them in the space provided.

1. _____
2. _____
3. _____
4. _____
5. _____

Now associate 6 through 10 and write them below:

6. _____
7. _____
8. _____
9. _____
10. _____

Now think back to your first ten memory pegs. See if you can close your eyes and repeat them in order.

Now write the next five:

11. _____
12. _____
13. _____
14. _____
15. _____

Finally, think again about each of your memory pegs and picture each. You're doing great! Five more and you will have proved to yourself that you can recall 20 items. Are you ready for your last five items? If so, write them below:

16. _____
17. _____
18. _____
19. _____
20. _____

MEMORY PEGS EXERCISE (Continued)

Here is your final test.

Write down the list provided on page 44 in the order you associated them with your memory pegs.

1. _____   11. _____

2. _____   12. _____

3. _____   13. _____

4. _____   14. _____

5. _____   15. _____

6. _____   16. _____

7. _____   17. _____

8. _____   18. _____

9. _____   19. _____

10. _____   20. _____

Were you able to get all 20 correct? If so, hurray for you. If not, repeat the exercise until you can recall every item in order. Then ask a friend to develop a new list for you. The more you practice using your memory peg system, the easier it will become to use this new mnemonic system you have developed.

MEMORY PEGS—SUMMARY

Think about what you have just done. At first this exercise may have seemed strange to you. However, if you were able to recall twenty items in order by association, you just proved to yourself that you possess the capacity for excellent memory skills.

This method of associating mental memory pegs may now be applied to memorizing the points in a sales talk, a speech, a report or any other business or personal activity.

Think about how much more confidence you will have when you know you have perfected a technique which will help you recall what you want to say. Simple, isn't it? That's all there is to it. A permanent storage place in your mind can be used when learning any series of new items.

When items are stored in an electronic computer, they are given a location in that machine's memory bank. When the machine is asked a question, the first task it has is to locate where the information has been stored. Like a computer, when you store the things you want to remember in their proper places, you will be able to recall them accurately.

Another way to think of your memory is to compare it to a safe deposit vault made up of rows of boxes. For instance, you might locate your first five memory pegs in the first five boxes. You must become familiar enough with your "locations" to recall that number four is a "table" (for example) and number 14 is a "bathroom mirror." When you are able to think of these memory pegs automatically, you can then recall any list of things you want to remember, in or out of sequence, backwards or forward!

Now, close your eyes and think again about the list on page 44. Is it still there? If so, go over it backwards and forward. Amazing, isn't it? Especially if you were able to recall every item.

Over time, with practice you will be able to mentally associate any item to your permanent memory pegs. Once you become proficient at this, you will be able to remember and retrieve information quickly and easily.

PART III—REMEMBERING NAMES AND NUMBERS

''Miss Smith, I'd like you to meet Mr. Edward Farquart, Mr. B. Oswald Tweeney, Mr. Reginald Von Liberwitz, Chief Running Water, Dr. Consuello Sitzmore and Bob Jones.''

REMEMBERING NAMES

It is good business to remember a person's name. Countless careers have been helped because an individual developed the ability to recall another person's name at a critical time.

A name is one of the most prized possessions a person has. A sense of worth is normally felt when another person has remembered your name, especially if that person was recently introduced to you for the first time. Because our identity is tied to our name, it is a compliment to have a person remember it.

Some individuals have displayed an exceptional ability to identify names. Napoleon is said to have remembered thousands of his soldiers by name. It has been reported that James A. Farley knew fifty thousand people by their first names. Charles Schwab, when manager of the Homestead Mill, earned the reputation of knowing by name each of his eight thousand employees. Charles E. Eliot, President of Harvard University for 40 years, reportedly knew every student by name. Some ''memory experts,'' using association systems, have developed an amazing ability to remember people's faces and names. One such expert, Harry Lorayne, can be introduced to hundreds of people entering a theater, one after the other, and then, facing the same people as an audience, give the name of any random person who rises.

Generally speaking it is easier to remember faces than names. All we have to do to remember a face is to recognize that we have seen it before. However, when we want to remember a name we need to recall a specific item without being given any clues. What we ultimately try to do is attach a name to a face, using the face as a clue to the name. You don't often hear people say—''Oh! I remember your name but not your face!''

Because of the difficulty many people have in remembering names, they develop a self-defeating attitude about their ability to recall names. People with this kind of attitude have a negative mental set about their recall. Often they refer to themselves as ''lousy'' at remembering names. You may hear them say, ''I'll never be able to remember names; I just can't do it.'' They picture themselves forgetting, and tell themselves over and over again, ''I don't have the ability to remember names.'' Their negative expectations influence their performance, and not remembering names becomes a self-fulfilling prophecy.

REMEMBERING NAMES (Continued)

If you want to improve your ability to remember names (or anything else for that matter), it is important to have a positive self-image. Replace the negative picture of yourself forgetting with one where you visualize yourself remembering people's names without difficulty. Such a scene might be a social gathering where you are introduced to eight people. When the host or hostess has completed the introductions, you might say, "let me make sure I have your names right," and then accurately repeat the eight names to the delight of all involved!

Along with a negative mental set, people usually don't remember names for one or more of the following reasons:

1. They are not interested in the people they are meeting and do not feel it is important enough to invest time and energy into remembering the name. This is probably the most important reason why people don't remember names. Without interest there is no motivation to remember. The bad news is that this "non-hearing" can carry over to situations where recalling a name is important.

2. Pre-occupation with other tasks at the time of introduction. This can be as simple as: hand-shaking, smiling, worrying about how you are coming across to the other person, planning what you will say, or anticipating the next person you will meet. When we are pre-occupied, a name will fail to register clearly.

3. The attitude, "I'll probably never meet this person again, so why bother; it really doesn't make any difference." However, often we do meet again. This results in people calling each other honey, fella, sweetie, dearie, Mac, champ and buddy.

4. Often we don't really forget the name. What happens is that we didn't hear it in the first place. Sometimes a person will mumble his or her name in such a way that you are unable to understand what that person said and are too embarrassed to say, "I didn't hear your name; will you repeat it?" Asking a person to repeat his or her name shows interest. It means that you want to make sure you get the name correct.

5. Names (especially those from different cultures) can be intangible and abstract. This can be a problem as they have no meaning to us. When names have some meaning to us (such as an old boy or girl friend), we are more apt to remember them.

REMEMBERING NAMES (Continued)

First Impressions

What happens when you first meet a person? It is normal to go through a mental process deciding how well they came across. Most of us form an immediate positive or negative opinion. This is called a first impression. It is important to be aware of how first impressions influence our desire to remember, or not remember a person's name.

One tip is to reshuffle your priorities at the time of the introduction. Do this by making a conscious effort to remember the name as a more important priority than letting first impressions block your ability to listen for the person's name.

Focus on the Person's Face

It is important to look directly at the person you are meeting and make eye contact. This can be difficult for several of us because society has become depersonalized in many respects. In addition, some of us may feel that it's impolite to look directly at another person's face. However, the opposite is true. Most people appreciate it when we look at them. By making eye contact, they feel we are interested in them. They normally respond to this attention by sending it back to us. Paying attention indicates that we want to remember their name. This by itself increases the likelihood you will work to remember a person's name.

Observe Carefully

Look carefully at the person you are meeting. Notice any unusual items such as the person's manner of talking, or physical features, etc. Listen carefully to the person's name and if unsure what you heard, ask the person to spell it. Repeat the name as often as possible without sounding phoney. Take a mental picture of the person and the name in your mind's eye.

SEVEN STEPS
TO REMEMBERING NAMES

SEVEN STEPS TO SUCCESS

Following is a simple seven step process to remember names:

1. Have a positive mental set.

2. Be interested in remembering each person's name.

3. Listen attentively and if unsure what it is, ask for a spelling.

4. Form an association to something you are familiar with (perhaps with someone else that has a similar name.)

5. Use the substitution process by substituting the name with a silly picture, or with something you're familiar with, such as:

   Ruth—Baby Ruth candy bar

   Bill—Thousand dollar bill

6. Link the silly picture to the person's name.

7. Repeat the name and substitution (or association) until you are confident you know it.

The above process forces you to listen, pay attention and concentrate. By putting these together along with substitution and/or association, your ability to remember names should measurably improve. The more you practice—the better you will become at remembering names.

Exercise Name	**Substitution**
Bob	Bobsled
Lily	Lily (the flower)

REMEMBERING NUMBERS

Most of us have jobs which make liberal use of numbers. In a given day there are dozens of opportunities to work with numbers. Often, our productivity would increase if we improved our ability to store and retrieve information such as phone numbers, prices, product code numbers, sales figures, computer codes, zip codes, dates, budget information and so forth.

As with other skills, some of us are better at recalling numbers than others. With practice however, we can all improve our current skill level.

Although only one formal system will be introduced in this book, there are several individual techniques we can develop to recall numbers. A few of these are:

- Looking for sequential combinations. For example the phone number for information is 555-1212. One way to remember it is to reorganize it as 555-12-12.

- Observing numbers within numbers. For instance, the zip code of some Florida towns is 31416, or Pi (3.1416).

- Paying attention to numbers that may be all odd or even, or that you can add together in an interesting way (i.e. 1, 348 may be learned as 1+3+4=8).

- Associating a number with a sports hero, famous date, birthday, etc.

Following is a more formal system to remember numbers. This system is a two-step process and works well with numbers containing at least seven digits. It involves transposing each digit in the number into a predetermined letter and then combining these letters to form words through the mental insertion of vowels between the letters. Once learned, a number can be recalled simply by remembering the word, or words, into which the numbers were transposed. The system depends totally upon the translation of each digit into a corresponding letter or sound each time it appears. This technique may have been invented by the great mathematician and philosopher Leibniz. He made use of it and commented favorably upon it.

THE SYSTEM

Because the English alphabet is a sound language, it can be broken into 10 sounds that are similar. There is no distinction between single and double letters. In this system, the vowels are disregarded. A, E, I, O, and U are not counted in the group. W, H, and Y are also not used. This system has the following letters and combinations joined to numbers.

Numbers	1	2	3	4	5	6	7	8	9	0
Letters/ Sounds	d t	n	m	r	l	soft g j ch, sh	hard g k	f v ph	b p	soft c s, z

REMEMBERING NUMBERS (Continued)

Numbers	1	2	3	4	5	6	7	8	9	0
Letters/ Sounds	d t	n	m	r	l	soft g j ch, sh	hard g k	f v ph	b p	soft c s, z

With this system it is possible to turn numbers into nonsense syllables, words, or phrases. For example, the number 302, 594 becomes ''Mason leaper'' (or, if one prefers, ''Miss Nelly Pry''), as follows:

Numbers	3	0	2	5	9	4
Letters	m	s	n	l	p	r

The number 3, 170, 850 will translate into ''my dog has fleas'':

Numbers	3	1	7	0	8	5	0
Letters	m	d	g	s	f	l	s

If a name is used, Mr. Orr translates into 4 and John Stroud would be 62-0141:

Letters	J	n	S	t	r	d
Numbers	6	2	0	1	4	1

Appointments can also be represented by numbers which are then translated into words or phrases. Thus, an appointment on Wednesday, the fourth day of the week, at three o'clock would become, first, 43 and then ''rhyme'':

Numbers	4	3
Letters	r	m

An appointment for April 16, at four o'clock becomes 4-16-4 and may be translated ''ride share'':

Numbers	4	1	6	4
Letters	r	d	sh	r

By learning this system and practicing daily, it is possible to replace and interpret the coded number translations to effectively remember a series of unrelated numbers.

This system is not for everybody. If you decide the system is worth learning, it is best to begin by selecting a few numbers you want to remember—such as your social security number, or some selected telephone numbers. The exercise on the facing page will allow you to experiment.

REMEMBERING NUMBERS—EXERCISE

To practice the memory device explained on page 53, transpose your bank account (or some similar number) with letters in the space below.

_____ _____ _____ - _____ _____ - _____ _____ _____ _____

Now, make the letters into a word or phrase that you can associate to your first memory peg.

Write in the space below six other numbers you want to remember (i.e. phone numbers you call most often.) Replace with letters, words or phrases in the space provided.

NUMBER	WORD OR PHRASE
1. _____	_____
2. _____	_____
3. _____	_____
4. _____	_____
5. _____	_____

This kind of exercise, done on a regular basis will amaze you by how quickly you develop the skill of replacing numbers with letters. Soon you will be able to remember easily a series of long, seemingly unrelated numbers.

PART IV—MEMORY EXERCISES & REVIEW

MEMORY EXERCISES

Following are a few memory exercises you can do on a daily basis that can assist you in improving your memory. Doing them can be enjoyable—so have fun! The secret is to practice them regularly, because "practice makes permanent."

1. While passing slowly through the same room, glance around attentively. Then in another room, try to recall as many objects you noted as possible. Put your entire energy into this exercise. Repeat every day for a week, and keep a record of the results. At the end of a week, compare your records and note your improvement.

2. When on the street observe objects around you. Having passed one block, recall as many objects as possible. Repeat every day for a week and note improvement.

3. Set your mental alarm clock. When you go to bed, tell yourself to awaken at a certain hour and see how close you awaken to the time you established. If you fail for a time, don't be discouraged. You will probably be impressed by how well you do. One tip, you must instantly arise at the appointed time or your self will discover you do not really mean what you told your mind to do. Continue until you have acquired the ability to awaken at any desired hour without the aid of an alarm clock.

4. In the morning resolve to recall a certain thought at an exact hour. Think with much concentration on this resolution and fix it firmly in your mind. Then dismiss it from immediate thought and attend to your other duties as usual. Do not try to keep the special thought in mind. At the end of the day, see if you remembered. In time you will learn to obey your own order. You may have some trouble at first but perseverance will make you master of keeping track of appointments this way. The reflex influence in other matters will appear in due time. Continue for at least six months.

5. Memorize some statistics that are of interest to you (i.e. the lifetime batting averages of some favorite ball players; the height of the five tallest mountains in the world; the distance to the nearest star, etc.) and for fun quote them to your friends.

MEMORY EXERCISES (Continued)

6. At the close of each day carefully review your thoughts and doings since morning.

   a. What were your most valuable ideas?

   b. What were your most intense sensations?

   c. What were your most important actions?

   Try to remember the positive ones so you can recall them when thinking about your future.

7. Make it a rule of life to learn some new and useful thing every day. Go outside of your daily doings or business for such information whenever possible.

8. Frequently commit to memory various lists. Make groupings of this information for future recall. Link each group with other groups from time to time. Make lists of items of public interest in your community, or historical information such as lists of capitols, counties, world leaders, local politicians, etc. Extend this exercise to fun things such as song lyrics, poems, etc.

9. Memorize the names and phone numbers of ten important customers, clients or co-workers.

SUMMARY REVIEW

SUMMARY REVIEW

Following is a review in the form of an elementary flow chart to help you remember the general principles presented earlier. Think about ways you can organize this information for even better recall, such as a memory map.

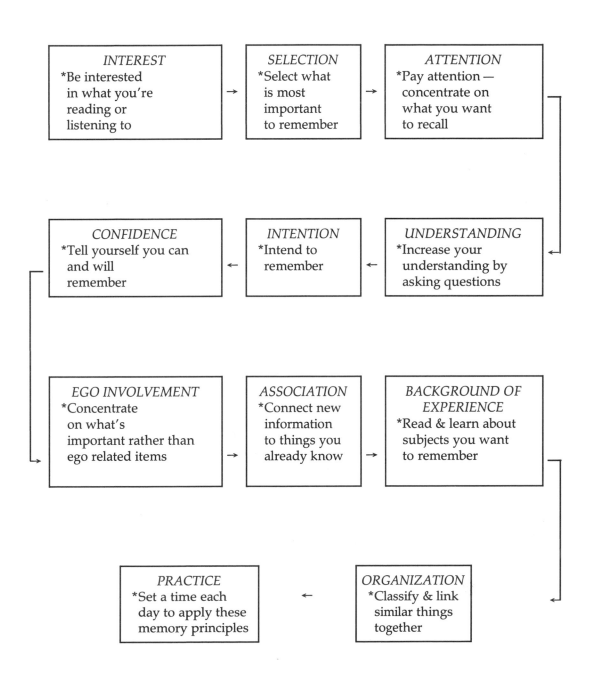

TEN RULES FOR SUCCESS

TEN RULES FOR SUCCESS

To improve your memory ability apply the following ten rules. If it helps, take this page of the book to your desk (or refrigerator) — any place you can review it often.

1. Make it a point to increase your original awareness by using your powers of observation and focus.

2. Concentrate on one thing at a time.

3. Visualize what you want to remember by forming pictures in your mind's eye. Concentrate on detail and "see" things in vivid color.

4. Build your self-confidence by re-reading pages 11 and 12 that discuss the potential of your brain and its unbelievable capability.

5. Substitute intangible or abstract information you wish to remember with something you can imagine. Associate this substitution to what you already know.

6. Link (in a ridiculous way if possible), one thing to another for easier recall.

7. Practice using your memory pegs. At first review them at least three times a day. Practice by associating 20 new objects on a regular basis and review your progress.

8. Apply the seven steps for remembering names described on page 52 each time you meet someone new.

9. Instead of using rote memory to recall a phone number, learn the system presented in this book and replace the numbers with letters. Do this on a daily basis until it becomes automatic.

10. Practice your memory exercises. Share them with family or friends. Make a game of memory improvement. You'll be delighted by the results.

Good luck!

REFERENCE

Bartlett, F.C. ''Remembering,'' London: Cambridge, U. Press 1932, Page 61, 110-112

Cemak, Laird S., *Improving Your Memory*, McGraw Hill 1976

Hersey, William D., *How to Cash In On Your Hidden Memory Power*, Prentice Hall, 1963

Lewis, David V., *How to Build Memory Skills*, Education for Management Inc., 1978

Logan, Arthur L., *''Remembering Made Easy''*, Arco Publishing Co., 1955

Weinland, James D., *How to Improve Your Memory*, Barnes Noble Books, Harper & Row, 1957

LIST OF OBJECTS SHOWN ON PAGE 20

> Although by no means exhaustive, following is a list of items shown in the picture on page 20. Check these against the list you made and then review the picture for others you may have spotted.

1. Four American flags
2. A chandelier
3. A stained glass window
4. Ceiling mouldings
5. Wainscotting
6. A long bar
7. A brass rail on the bar
8. A cash register behind the bar
9. A large glass mirror behind the bar
10. A lamp behind the bar
11. Several different size bottles behind the bar
12. A cat behind the bar
13. A bar tender in an apron behind the bar
14. A person in street clothes behind the bar
15. Five plates on the bar
16. One bottle on the bar
17. Two wine glasses on the bar
18. Two regular glasses on the bar
19. A black man in a bowler hat at the bar
20. A man drinking at the bar
21. A man handing a glass to the man behind the bar
22. A man holding an object at the far end of the bar
23. A bar rail under the bar
24. A spitoon under the bar rail
25. A man walking toward the bar
26. Two men near the far wall in the bar
27. A man with his hands in his pockets, smoking a pipe
28. A man reading a newspaper near the far wall
29. A wooden plank floor
30. A tapestry against the far wall
31. Signature of the artist bottom right of picture
32. Add your own: _____
33. _____
34. _____
35. _____

AUTHOR RESPONSE
VISUAL or AUDITORY—from page 25

Which are you?

Copy your ratings from the exercise on page 25. Add up your scores in each category. The higher score will indicate which skill is more developed for you at this time.

VISUAL	AUDITORY
1a. _____	1b. _____
2. _____	3. _____
4. _____	5. _____
6. _____	7. _____
8. _____	9. _____
10. _____	11. _____
12. _____	13. _____
14. _____	15. _____
16. _____	17. _____
TOTAL _____	_____

I seem to be more of an _____ learner. Would your friends agree?

NOTES

NOTES

NOTES

NOTES

NOTES

NOTES

NOTES

NOW AVAILABLE FROM CRISP PUBLICATIONS

Books • Videos • CD Roms • Computer-Based Training Products

If you enjoyed this book, we have great news for you. There are over 200 books available in the *50-Minute*™ Series. To request a free full-line catalog, contact your local distributor or Crisp Publications, Inc., 1200 Hamilton Court, Menlo Park, CA 94025. Our toll-free number is 800-442-7477. Visit our website at http://www.crisp-pub.com.

Subject Areas Include:

Management

Human Resources

Communication Skills

Personal Development

Marketing/Sales

Organizational Development

Customer Service/Quality

Computer Skills

Small Business and Entrepreneurship

Adult Literacy and Learning

Life Planning and Retirement

CRISP WORLDWIDE DISTRIBUTION

English language books are distributed worldwide. Major international distributors include:

ASIA/PACIFIC

Australia/New Zealand: In Learning, PO Box 1051, Springwood QLD, Brisbane, Australia 4127   Tel: 61-7-3-841-2286, Facsimile: 61-7-3-841-1580
ATTN: Messrs. Gordon

Singapore: 85, Genting Lane, Guan Hua Warehouse Bldng #05-01, Singapore 349569   Tel: 65-749-3389, Facsimile: 65-749-1129
ATTN: Evelyn Lee

Japan: Phoenix Associates Co., LTD., Mizuho Bldg. 3-F, 2-12-2, Kami Osaki, Shinagawa-Ku, Tokyo 141   Tel: 81-33-443-7231, Facsimile: 81-33-443-7640
ATTN: Mr. Peter Owans

CANADA

Reid Publishing, Ltd., Box 69559-109 Thomas Street, Oakville, Ontario Canada L6J 7R4.   Tel: (905) 842-4428, Facsimile: (905) 842-9327
ATTN: Mr. Stanley Reid

Trade Book Stores: *Raincoast Books*, 8680 Cambie Street, Vancouver, B.C., V6P 6M9   Tel: (604) 323-7100, Facsimile: (604) 323-2600
ATTN: Order Desk

EUROPEAN UNION

England: *Flex Training*, Ltd. 9-15 Hitchin Street, Baldock, Hertfordshire, SG7 6A, England   Tel: 44-1-46-289-6000, Facsimile: 44-1-46-289-2417
ATTN: Mr. David Willetts

INDIA

Multi-Media HRD, Pvt., Ltd., National House, Tulloch Road, Appolo Bunder, Bombay, India 400-039   Tel: 91-22-204-2281, Facsimile: 91-22-283-6478
ATTN: Messrs. Aggarwal

SOUTH AMERICA

Mexico: *Grupo Editorial Iberoamerica*, Nebraska 199, Col. Napoles, 03810 Mexico, D.F.   Tel: 525-523-0994, Facsimile: 525-543-1173
ATTN: Señor Nicholas Grepe

SOUTH AFRICA

Alternative Books, Unit A3 Micro Industrial Park, Hammer Avenue, Stridom Park, Randburg, 2194 South Africa   Tel: 27-11-792-7730, Facsimile: 27-11-792-7787
ATTN: Mr. Vernon de Haas